This book belongs to the
Children's Corner Library
One World Market

Gift of *Laurel Ratsoy*

Date *June 2000*

1918 Perry Street, Durham, NC   919-286-2457

Young Artists of the World™
Taiwan

Lisa Lin's Painting: "Making Mooncakes"

Jacquiline Touba, Ph.D. and Barbara Glasser

in collaboration with the IACA World Awareness Children's Museum

The Rosen Publishing Group's

New York

The young artist's drawing was submitted to the International Youth Art Exchange program of the IACA World Awareness Children's Museum. You are invited to contribute your artwork to the museum.
For more details, write to the IACA World Awareness Children's Museum, 227 Glen Street, Glens Falls, NY 12801.
Acknowledgments: Karen Hess.

Published in 1997 by The Rosen Publishing Group, Inc.
29 East 21st Street, New York, NY 10010

First Edition

Book Design: Erin McKenna

Photo Credits: p. 4 © Phyllis Picardi/International Stock Photography; p. 7 © Cliff Hollenbeck/International Stock Photography; p. 8 © M. Spector/H. Armstrong Roberts, Inc.; p. 12 © Jim Hays/MIDWESTOCK; p. 16 © Bill Stanton/International Stock Photography; p. 19 © Don Wolf/MIDWESTOCK; p. 20 © Bettmann.

Touba, Jacquiline.
    Taiwan: Lisa Lin's painting "Making mooncakes" / by Jacquiline Touba and Barbara Glasser.
        p.   cm. — (Young artists of the world)
    Includes index.
    Summary: The young Taiwanese artist, Lisa Lin, describes her painting of her family making mooncakes for the Mid–Autumn Festival.
    ISBN 0-8239-5104-9 (lib.bdg.)
    1. Taiwan—Social life and customs—1975–   —Juvenile literature. 2. Mid–Autumn Festival—Juvenile literature. 3. Children's art—Taiwan. 4. Lin, Lisa. 5. Taiwan—Social life and customs. [1. Mid–Autumn Festival. 2. Childrens' art. 3. Lin, Lisa.] I. Glasser, Barbara. II. Lin, Lisa. III. Title. IV. Series.
    DS799.845.T68 1997
    951.24'9—dc21
                                                        96–37695
                                                          CIP
                                                           AC

Manufactured in the United States of America

Contents

My Family

My name is Lisa Lin. I am from **Taiwan** (ty-WHAN). I have a little sister named Ya-wen. I have a little brother named Tse-che. Many years ago, my grandparents came to Taiwan from a nearby country called China. They like to tell us stories about when they lived in China. My grandparents take care of my brother and sister when my parents are at work. My mother and father work for the same company.

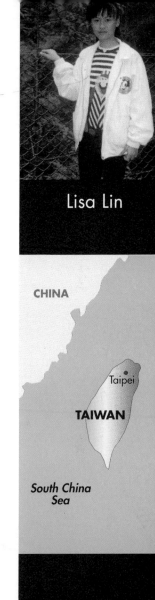

Lisa Lin

CHINA

Taipei

TAIWAN

South China Sea

◀ My grandmother teaches me about my history, just like this grandmother teaches her grandchildren.

5

My City

Lisa's dog, Lai Foo, is an important member of the family.

We live in the town of **Hsin Chuang** (sheen joo-ang). Hsin Chuang is near **Taipei** (ty-PAY). Taipei is the **capital** (KAP-ih-tul) of Taiwan. Hsin Chuang once had many farms and large fields. Now it is more like a city. But we still have trees and open spaces where I walk my dog. My dog's name is Lai Foo. Lai Foo means "Good Luck" in Chinese or "Lucky" in English. When I visit Taipei with my family, Lai Foo stays at home.

Taipei is the capital of Taiwan, and is a ▶ very busy city full of many people.

My Country

Taiwan is an island. It is near the countries of Korea, Japan, and the Philippines.

There are many mountains and green forests in Taiwan. These forests are mostly on the center of the island. There are **plains** (PLAYNZ) and cities on other parts of the island.

Many people came to Taiwan from China during the 1940s and 1950s. They brought their **language** (LANG-widge) with them. It is called Chinese. The people who lived in Taiwan before the Chinese still live in the mountains and on the plains.

Lisa's painting shows one of the many trees that grow in the forests of Taiwan.

◀ Taroko Gorge is one of the many beautiful places on the island of Taiwan.

9

My Painting

I painted this picture when I was twelve years old. It shows my family making mooncakes. The mooncakes are for the Mid-Autumn Moon Festival. The Mid-Autumn Moon Festival **celebrates** (SEL-uh-brayts) the biggest and brightest full moon of the year. This moon comes at the time of the year when people **harvest** (HAHR-vest) their crops. Crops are foods that are grown to eat or to sell at markets.

We grow rice and bananas at our house. Rice is one of my favorite foods.

Lisa's family enjoys making mooncakes for the Mid-Autumn Moon Festival. ▶

The Moon Calendar

The Mid-Autumn Moon Festival is held in the fall. The day of the festival is the fifteenth day of the eighth month of the **lunar** (LOO-ner) calendar. The lunar calendar is used by many people around the world. It follows the **phases** (FAY-zez) of the moon. With the lunar calendar, the months of the year are at different times each year. That means the Mid-Autumn Festival may be in September one year and at other times it may be in October or November. It is always a time of joy and celebration for all of us.

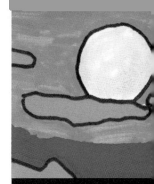

The phase of the moon that shines during the Mid-Autumn Moon Festival is one of the biggest of the entire year.

◀ The lunar calendar, based on the phases of the moon, is used by different people all over the world.

13

My grandmother used to make mooncakes with her mother when she was a little girl.

Making Mooncakes

Making mooncakes for the Mid-Autumn Moon Festival is fun for everyone in my family. My picture shows my mother using a rolling pin to flatten the outside part of the mooncake. My grandmother is rolling the filling that will go inside. The filling is made of all sorts of good food, such as dates, red beans, and pineapple. I am stuffing the mooncakes with my favorite filling, egg yolks in red bean paste.

We will make many mooncakes in one day. We give them to our friends and family. But we eat many of them ourselves!

Everyone in Lisa's family takes part in the making of the mooncakes. ▶

Eating Mooncakes

My little sister is excited about the mooncakes. She knows how delicious they will taste after they are cooked. She puts them in her basket to take to the kitchen. My dog, Lai Foo, is hoping he will get some mooncakes, too.

After the mooncakes are cooked, we will take them to the park. Then the festival will begin. Many families come to the park. We eat mooncakes, sing, and celebrate the Mid-Autumn Moon Festival together.

Lisa's sister can't wait to eat mooncakes at the Festival.

◀ Festivals are important to families and children in Taiwan.

17

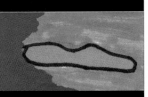

Do you see Lady Chang-Eh riding across the sky in Lisa's painting?

The Festival

The Mid-Autumn Moon Festival is very special to me. The festival comes from a story about **Lady Chang-Eh** (LAY-dee chung-uh). Lady Chang-Eh tasted her husband's secret drink for living a long life. She instantly became **immortal** (im-MOR-tuhl) and flew up to the moon. On the night of the festival, we watch the moon while we eat our mooncakes. We hope to see Lady Chang-Eh riding across the sky.

An important part of the Mid-Autumn Moon Festival is watching the night sky for Lady Chang-Eh. ▶

Harvest Time

In many parts of the world, people celebrate the harvest time. In Taiwan, we grow rice, sugarcane, tea, bananas, and pineapple for the harvest.

The Mid-Autumn Moon Festival is held after the harvest. In Taiwan, major festivals usually happen before and after the planting of crops, and after the crops are harvested. The festivals are always full of music and singing. Everyone is happy at harvest time.

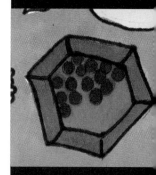

Lisa's painting shows some of the things that are harvested and used in the making of mooncakes.

◀ Rice is an important harvest crop in many parts of Asia.

21

A Chinese Greeting

A traditional greeting in Taiwan for "Hello, how are you?" is "*chih-fan-le-meiyo*" (che-fan-le-may-yoo). This means "Have you eaten yet?" You can see how important food is to us!

One day, maybe you and your family will visit Taiwan. You can eat mooncakes with my family and me. We can celebrate the Mid-Autumn Moon Festival together. I would like that very much.

Glossary

capital (KAP-ih-tul) The leading city of a state or country.

celebrate (SEL-uh-brayt) To enjoy a special time in honor of something or someone.

chih-fan-le-meiyo (che-fan-le-may-yoo) A Chinese greeting that means "Have you eaten yet?"

harvest (HAHR-vest) The picking and gathering of food grown on farms.

Hsin Chuang (sheen joo-ang) A town near Taipei.

immortal (im-MOR-tuhl) Living forever.

Lady Chang-Eh (LAY-dee chung-uh) An imaginary woman who is part of the moon festival story.

language (LANG-widge) The words people use to speak.

lunar (LOO-ner) Having to do with the moon.

phase (FAYZ) One of the changing parts of a cycle.

plains (PLAYNZ) Long, flat areas of land.

Taipei (ty-PAY) The capital of Taiwan.

Taiwan (ty-WHAN) An island near China.

Index